QUIET

HAUNTINGS

Quiet Hauntings

A play by

Simon Kurt Unsworth

BLACK
SHUCK
BOOKS

First published in Great Britain in 2024 by
Black Shuck Books
Kent, UK

Quiet Hauntings © Simon Kurt Unsworth, 2024

Set in Caslon by WHITEspace
www.white-space.uk

Cover design by Sarah Edwards
Cover photo by Chris Erdman
Interior layout © WHITEspace, 2024
Cover image courtesy of The Wellcome Collection

978-1-913038-90-8

For Rosie, director of more than just the play, and to all the cast and crew who made Quiet Hauntings *such fun to write, create, edit and perform. You can all have a rest now.*

Dramatis Personae

JUDGE MYERS	A Judge
THE ACCUSED	A young criminal
RICHARD MURDOCH	A academic specialising in parapsychological studies
ALICE TIDYMAN	A defence barrister
JAMES COLLINS	A prosecution barrister
DANIELLE	A young woman
ROB	Danielle's father
THE HOTELIER	The manager of the Forest Lodge Hotel
A POLICEMAN	The Arm of the Law
THE WOMAN	A ghost
MEGAN	A widow
ARNOST	An M.C.
PEG	A ghost
JUROR 1	A juror
JUROR 2	A juror
JUROR 3	A juror
JUROR 4	A juror
JUROR 5	A juror
JUROR 6	A juror
FARMER	An apparition

PROLOGUE

TIDYMAN and THE ACCUSED are on the stage,
seated in chairs.

TIDYMAN

We cannot use that as a defence.

THE ACCUSED

Why not?

TIDYMAN

Because they'll laugh you out of the court and straight into the cell.

THE ACCUSED

But it's the truth. I thought I was supposed to tell the truth.

TIDYMAN

Ah, the naivety of youth. No, son, the truth is not always the best road to take. In this case, it would a mistake. Sometimes, a dignified silence is better.

THE ACCUSED

But I've not got any other truth to tell. How can I get anywhere if you won't let me tell the truth? Because I wouldn't have done it if the stuff I'm not supposed to talk about hadn't happened.

TIDYMAN

We're going around in circles. I have to pull a defence together to try to get the jurors to see you as something other than a young thug who murdered someone in cold blood—

THE ACCUSED

I didn't!

TIDYMAN

—and then fled the scene rather than attempting to provide any kind of assistance. Do you see my problem? Because that's the position the prosecution will take, trust me.

THE ACCUSED

So what do I do?

TIDYMAN

Let me ask you a few questions. Please don't be offended by any of them, and answer them truthfully. What you tell me might help.

THE ACCUSED

Okay.

TIDYMAN

You went to the farm with the specific intention of robbing it?

THE ACCUSED

Yes.

TIDYMAN

Why? Why there, I mean?

THE ACCUSED

Because I thought there'd be stuff worth having. Not money but stuff like tools, stuff I could sell on quick. Why that one? Because it looked easy. No big family, not many workers at this time of year. Quick in, quick out.

TIDYMAN

And were you drunk?

THE ACCUSED

No.

TIDYMAN

Or on drugs?

THE ACCUSED

No.

TIDYMAN

Do you drink or take drugs generally?

THE ACCUSED

No. Well, I drink. Sometimes. Not a lot, and never when I'm out.

TIDYMAN

Out?

THE ACCUSED

On a job. Working.

TIDYMAN

A small tip – don't describe your activities as a 'job' or 'work' on the stand. It'll make the jurors think you're being flippant.

THE ACCUSED

Flippant?

TIDYMAN

Taking the piss.

THE ACCUSED

Okay.

TIDYMAN

What's your mood when you go out to burgle somewhere?

THE ACCUSED

I don't know. I mean, I don't think about it.

TIDYMAN

Well, are you excited? Scared? Happy?

THE ACCUSED

Usually a bit hyper, on edge, but nothing serious. Being a bit on edge, it's useful, it's like it's a way of focussing.

TIDYMAN

And there was nothing unusual about this time?

THE ACCUSED

Not until I started seeing the stuff I saw and hearing the stuff I heard, no.

TIDYMAN

And you've never experienced anything like that before?

THE ACCUSED

No. I don't even believe in it. Well, I didn't. I do now.

TIDYMAN

And you did what you did because—

THE ACCUSED

Because I was piss scared! I'd been chased about the place by things I couldn't understand, that couldn't even be real, and I kept on going because they were all behind me and I couldn't see a way back without going through them all again and it was getting worse because every room I went in something happened and then I was in that last room and... and...

THE ACCUSED Breaks down, covers face, cries, etc. TIDYMAN looks on impassive – their job is not to comfort or absolve but to understand and to construct a defence. Eventually, THE ACCUSED quietens, pulls themselves together.

TIDYMAN
And then you killed the farmer.

THE ACCUSED
Yes. I didn't think he was real, though. I swear, I thought that it was another of those things, like the girl with no eyes that had followed me along the hallway screaming, things that couldn't be real, and I was so scared and I just lashed out because I wanted it to go away, to leave me alone! I just wanted them to leave me alone!

THE ACCUSED is getting upset as they relate this, backing away, possibly even crashing their chair over backwards – TIDYMAN still does not react except to make notes.

TIDYMAN
You've not mentioned a child with no eyes before.

THE ACCUSED
Would you? I know no one believes me about the stuff I've already told them, that everyone thinks I'm bullshitting or mad or something, but it's all true, I swear. All of it. Every bit.

TIDYMAN

And you'll say that in front of a judge and jury if you need
to?

THE ACCUSED

Of course. It's the truth.

TIDYMAN

God, I must be mad. It *is* mad.

*TIDYMAN thinks, makes an occasional note. There is
a long pause – at one point THE ACCUSED makes a
noise as though to say something and TIDYMAN holds
up a hand to stop them.*

TIDYMAN

(*more to themselves than anyone, just thinking aloud*)
We can't just have you sit there and tell it, can we? There's
no context, it's just a story, a fiction, just… what did you
say… just bullshit. I'd have to show that other people have
had the same reactions, seen or heard the same things,
wouldn't I? I don't need proof, just to plant a seed. No,
that's not right, not me, I can't plant it. So, someone else.
But who? Never mind, get to that later, that's the easy part,
for now what? What? Think, dammit.

*Another pause, more note taking, then TIDYMAN
clearly comes to a conclusion, shuts their notebook and
faces THE ACCUSED.*

TIDYMAN

Well, if you're determined, I don't know that we've any
better path available to us. I'm not sure it's got a chance
in Hell of working, but maybe we can unsettle their case
enough for a hung jury, or at least some debate, maybe get

the judge on our side for a more reasonable sentence. So, go on then.

THE ACCUSED
Go on what?

TIDYMAN
Tell me. Tell me everything.

THE ACCUSED
Everything?

TIDYMAN
Everything. Tell me about the ghosts.

ACT I
Scene I

[Note: sections performed on the stage are marked 'FS' – otherwise, performed from the lower staging at the stage front]

Woman seated behind a desk – Judge MYERS. Three people face them: TIDYMAN (defence barrister), COLLINS (prosecution barrister) and MURDOCH.

MYERS

I have to admit a little confusion, which is why I've called you in to this meeting. It's not a formal pre-trial meeting, you understand, just a little informal get together so you, Mr Tidyman, can explain exactly what you're playing at.

TIDYMAN

Playing at, Judge Myers? I would have thought it was fairly obvious. My request isn't so outlandish, after all. I simply want to call an expert witness.

MYERS

An expert witness who you want to tell ghost stories in my court?

TIDYMAN

No. Well, yes, but for a reason.

COLLINS

Your honour, if I—

MYERS

You'll get your turn in a minute, Mr Collins.

MURDOCH

Perhaps I can—

MYERS

Ah, ah, no also, Mr Murdoch. Mr Tidyman, you have precisely one minute. Then, and only then, if it's appropriate, I'll ask you to contribute, Mr Murdoch. Now, shall we?

TIDYMAN

Your honour, my client is accused of murder. That he killed the man in the commission of a robbery he doesn't deny, but his contention is that something in the house spooked him, scared him so badly that he was no longer able to think rationally. He believed, at the point of the attack, that the sudden appearance of the victim was not the appearance of a human but, well, a ghost or supernatural entity, and in his mind he was only defending himself from this entity.

COLLINS

So it's a madness defence?

TIDYMAN

Not at all, my client wasn't in any way insane. He was, however, terrified and reacted proportionate to the level of his terror. We're simply asking for the court to consider the possibility that my client's reaction to the building may have contributed to tragic outcome of the situation, and would ask that a lesser charge be considered. In support of this, I have asked Mr Murdoch here, a highly regarded academic with many years research in precisely this field, to present to the court other provable instances where people in certain places responded to unusual feelings or stimuli, so that the jury can understand that it's not an unreasonable reaction that my client had.

Projected rear of the stage an advert appears:

Have you seen a ghost? Had an experience you cannot explain? If so, serious researcher would like to hear from you. No timewasters. Must be prepared to go on record. Contact: Richard Murdoch:
richardmurdochghosts@gmail.com

Image remains throughout next section.

COLLINS
Oh for God's—

Breaks off as MYERS looks sternly at him, takes a breath, continues.

COLLINS
I'm sorry, but you're honestly expecting us to accept that your client was influenced by a ghost? That he panicked and killed the owner of the farmhouse he'd broken into because he was frightened of a floating bedsheet going 'woooooo'?

TIDYMAN
No, I'm asking that the jury be allowed to consider the idea that from the moment he trespassed onto the farmland, even before he broke into the cattle sheds or house, my client was exposed to a barrage of what Mr Murdoch describes as 'psychic stimuli', ultimately leading him into a fight or flight panic response far more severe than any usually experienced.

MURDOCH
Also, ghosts never look like that, and they don't go 'woo'.

MYERS

Ah, so we turn to you, Mr Murdoch. Your resumé and research history are, admittedly, very good but I'm still unclear. Do you expect to prove the existence of ghosts in my courthouse?

MURDOCH

No, your honour, just the existence of interactions between people and places, quiet places where people can hear things they wouldn't normally hear, see things they wouldn't normally see, leading to fear, anger, sadness, whatever. We've already run tests on the young man and his scores indicate a level of psychic ability above the average, and I'd like the opportunity to show how his response to the building might have been triggered by something most of us can't see or feel.

COLLINS

This is preposterous, your honour, please tell me you aren't considering this?

MYERS

Are you telling me which way I ought to conclude this discussion, Mr Collins?

COLLINS

No, your honour, but surely—

MYERS

Surely what? It seems to me that if the defence is adamant that a central plank of their argument is to be a reaction to, what did you call them Mr Tidyman, 'psychic stimuli', then they should be allowed at least some opportunity to try to explain and/or prove this to the jury. Mr Murdoch, you're happy to be listed in court documents as an expert witness in ghosts?

MURDOCH

No, your honour, but an expert witness in Parapsychogical Studies would be acceptable.

COLLINS

Your honour—

MYERS

Enough, Mr Collins. Call your own debunker if you must, but for now I think I'll have silence. Mr Tidyman, this is highly unorthodox but I can't deny your right to try it, despite the damage you risk doing to your reputation. I am minded, in this instance, to take a leap. Do not make me regret this, Mr Tidyman, nor you, Mr Murdoch.

TIDYMAN

Many thanks, your honour, and we won't. Richard, over to you...

TIDYMAN and MYERS leave the Apron. MURDOCH takes a seat behind the now vacated desk. The advert remains projected for several long moments and then the silence is broken by the sound of a telephone ringing which gradually fades to nothing. Advert vanishes.

FS (enter left) DANIELLE. Her father, ROB, enters from stage right. Sound effects of an after school day – cars, voices, etc.

DANIELLE

Dad, why are you here? Is Mum okay? What's wrong?

ROB

Mum's fine and you know what's wrong, darling. Me and your mum, it's...

DANIELLE

Yeah, I heard. All the neighbours heard, too. For the whole weekend. I think the people in the next town heard. We're all used to hearing it now, though. But why are you here? I don't need picking up from school. I'm not a child.

ROB

I know you're not, but it wasn't a great weekend was it? I thought I'd make it up to you, so you and me, we're going away for a couple of nights. Your mum, she needs a break. She needs some quiet time.

DANIELLE

A break from me?

ROB

From everything, Danny. From everything.

DANIELLE

But what about school?

ROB

Ah, I'll square that. You're doing okay, a couple of days won't hurt you. Besides, there's more to life than books and facts and homework. Come on. Time's a'wasting.

They turn and go to stage right. ROB disappears offstage but DANIELLE comes down to the Apron where MURDOCH is seated behind the desk, a pad and several sets of notes in front of him. DANIELLE knocks.

MURDOCH

Come in, please.

DANIELLE

Hello.

MURDOCH

It's Danielle? We spoke on the phone, yes? Thank you so much for coming to see me. You're still happy to tell me your story? To go on record?

DANIELLE

Yes.

MURDOCH places a small digital recorder on the table and turns it on.

MURDOCH

Well, then. Tell me your story…

Scene II – Forest Lodge

DANIELLE

My mum and dad always argued. You know some people argue and then make up, all the time, arguing so that they can just have the making up part? Well, that wasn't mum and dad. No, they'd argue and then there'd be a horrible silence in the house for days, and then her and dad would use me as a go-between. I used to wonder why they were married at all and then I'd think, *It's me, they're together and unhappy because of me. I'm making them unhappy.*

MURDOCH

That can't have been easy.

DANIELLE

Well, I didn't know any different. It was life. Anyway, when Dad picked me up from school and took me away that day I was surprised, but not *really* surprised. He'd always treat me to something after an argument, as though he had to make it up to me, as though it was his job because Mum was the moodier one. She held her grudges longer, Dad would just lose his temper and shout but could be pretending nothing had happened within a few minutes as long as you didn't keep on about stuff. The bigger the argument, the bigger the treat – and it was always something that got us out of the house: a trip to the cinema, a pizza in a nice restaurant, that sort of thing. So a few days in a hotel wasn't a surprise, even if it was unusual.

MURDOCH

And which hotel was it?

FS: ROB walks on stage left and crosses to where the HOTELIER has appeared stage right.

HOTELIER

Welcome to the Forest Lodge Hotel sir! The finest small hotel in the Lake District! If you'd just like to sign the register and fill in the details on the form, I'll show you to your room. I assume it's a twin room you're wanting. The young lady...?

ROB

My daughter, don't worry. And a twin is fine.

HOTELIER

Excellent. Come this way.

They exit Stage right.

DANIELLE

It was in the lakes, small but grand with lots of dark wood panels. It was at the end of a long road, almost at the top of a hill, and it looked down over one of the lakes. The view was beautiful.

MURDOCH

Can I ask, just for the record, when this took place?

DANIELLE

Ten years ago, so I was about 14, but if you're worried about my memory, don't be. I remember everything very clearly.

ROB and HOTELIER come to side of apron and the two of them along with DANIELLE go upstairs onto stage as DANIELLE carries on.

DANIELLE

Our room was on the first floor, but the stairs turned back on themselves on the way up and there was one of those balcony sections, an... an...

MURDOCH

A mezzanine?

DANIELLE

Yes, a mezzanine, that's it! Anyway, on the wall of the mezzanine was an old portrait of a couple. They both looked very stern.

ROB, HOTELIER and DANIELLE stop as a picture appears projected onto the stage rear of a couple dressed in old fashioned, fine clothes.

HOTELIER

That's the Roses. They built this place in the late nineteenth century and ran it until my grandfather bought it from them just after World War One. You're staying in the Charlotte suite, which is named after their daughter.

They carry on. The picture fades, replaced by one of a young woman also in fine clothes, looking miserable. She has dark hair. As the trio depart offstage, presumably into the Charlotte Suite, the picture remains before also fading. At the picture's bottom are the dates 1902 – 1919.

DANIELLE returns to the apron and sits again.

DANIELLE

We unpacked and Dad fell asleep on the bed so I looked around the room. It was nice but a bit old fashioned. Floral, you know? Charlotte's picture was on the wall and she looked as miserable as her parents did in their picture. There was a little plaque on the frame of the picture, at the bottom, with dates on. She'd died in 1919, so she'd only been young. Seventeen, I think. I didn't like that, not at all.

MURDOCH
Was there something specific you didn't like about it?

DANIELLE
That she'd been so young, I think. She was older than me, but not much. It made me feel uncomfortable.

MURDOCH
I see. I'm sorry, I interrupted. Please, carry on.

DANIELLE
After a while I got hungry but I knew Dad'd be grumpy if I woke him. I had a book in my bag so I went and sat in one the chairs and thought I might as well read.

DANIELLE pulls chair from desk and positions it near stage, sits in it and opens her book. Her back is to the stage.

As she speaks this next section the GHOST appears from the back of the stage – initially simply standing at the rear in shadow, revealed as the spotlight slowly increases, and then she moves slowly across it, towards DANIELLE. In appearance it is female, shrouded not in clothes but a mass of white, tattered cloth like muslin or curtain lace that is wrapped around her. Its face is covered except for one eye, and we can see that its hair is probably dark. Its feet are bare. Any visible skin is very pale and has mud and dirty marks on it. As she nears DANIELLE the vague sound of dripping water can be heard.

DANIELLE
I was on the sofa when I felt suddenly that there was someone else in the room, someone staring at me, and

the feeling wouldn't go away. Someone was staring at me, studying me like I was some fascinating thing they had just found. I remember being too frightened to move, although frightened of what I didn't know. Of the gaze. Of the eyes. I started to hear something, like the sounds of water dripping. I was so cold. I wanted to do something, to do anything to wake Dad, but I couldn't. It was like I was in a bubble that contained just me and this other person

She shuts the book.

DANIELLE
Then I saw her for the first time, just in the corner of my eye, so close to me, leaning over me, studying me and I still couldn't move.

(FS) The GHOST is now on its hands and knees at the front of the stage, head very close to DANIELLE'S but tilted as though, yes, it's studying her with its one visible eye. Slowly, as DANIELLE talks, it reaches up, holds one trembling hand towards DANIELLE's face.

DANIELLE
I couldn't breathe. I didn't know if it was a madwoman or the ghost of Charlotte or what but I couldn't move then—

The GHOST reaches out one finger and touches DANIELLE'S cheek.

DANIELLE
(screams, loud and very sudden)

ROB
(offstage, waking up)
What? What?

GHOST scuttles back, leaves stage as ROB emerges and rushes to DANIELLE on the apron

ROB

Jesus, what's wrong?

DANIELLE throws her arms around ROB'S neck and clings to him.

DANIELLE

Dad, there was...there was… a woman.

ROB

What? What do you mean, a woman?

DANIELLE

In the room. She… she…

ROB

Ah, baby girl, you fell asleep. Travelling's always tiring and you fell asleep and had a bad dream. Look, there's no one here.

They look around. ROB goes up onto the stage as he speaks and makes a show of checking the door, looking behind things, etc.

ROB

There's nothing here, Danny. You had a dream, that's all.

DANIELLE

But…

ROB

There's *nothing* Danny. Nothing at all. Well, you've woken us both up. We may as well wash up and go and get some food.

DANIELLE

Okay.

ROB leaves

DANIELLE brings the chair back over to MURDOCH and sits.

DANIELLE

But it wasn't nothing, and I hadn't been asleep, and where the ghost or whatever it was touched me I had a mark. The touch was cold, the coldest thing I've ever felt, so cold it burned. I've still got the mark, look.

She shows MURDOCH her cheek which now has a faint mark on it. A photo of DANIELLE with a scarred cheek appears on the rear projection, like a police evidence photo.

MURDOCH

I see it. It's not like any kind of scar I've seen before. It's almost like an old burn.

DANIELLE

It doesn't hurt, not after the actual touch, it never has. It's just a mark. I've never had it checked out. I usually cover it with makeup but I thought you'd probably want to see it.

MURDOCH

Yes. Thank you. What happened next?

DANIELLE

We went for dinner. Dad was doing his pretend everything was fine routine, but I mentioned to the manager that Charlotte had died young.

CHARLOTTE's picture fades up again.

HOTELIER
(FS)

Well, she didn't die. I mean, obviously, she did, but they never found a body so they just assumed it. Some people thought she'd run away, because the Roses were very strict and Charlotte wanted to live her own life, that she went into the forest, changed her outfit and ran off. They found her dress all muddy and torn a few months later, that was the only sign of her. Other people thought she'd run into a soldier, just home and demob happy and maybe drunk, and he'd done something to her, killed her and let the lake have her. There was no evidence of that, but you know what rumours are like. She was never seen again, I know that.

DANIELLE

That's awful!

HOTELIER

Yes. We had a séance here once and some spirit came through claiming to be Charlotte, but you never know with those things, do you?

ROB
(FS)

Speaking of spirits, I'll have a whiskey I think. Make it a decent one, eh?

HOTELIER

Certainly. We have a fine selection – come with me and I'll show you what we've got.

They leave

DANIELLE

And that was that. I went back to the room alone because once Dad was drinking whiskey he'd be there for ages. I lit all the lights in the room and read for a bit and eventually went to bed. I thought it'd be hard to fall asleep, that I'd be scared, but I wasn't, and I was asleep before Dad came back.

MURDOCH

And nothing happened that night?

DANIELLE

No. It was fine. The next morning Dad insisted, absolutely insisted, that we go for a walk. We had to, he said, because we were in such a beautiful part of the world. It'll be something to tell Mum about, he said, although I never would because it'd be like rubbing her nose in it, you know? Hey, we went somewhere really nice Mum, and spent money that the family can't really afford, and we all know that because half the arguments are about money, while you stayed at home but don't worry I can describe it for you. You know?

MURDOCH

Yes.

DANIELLE

So we went for a walk around the lake. It was one of those little ones that sit high up in the hills that not as many people go to, so it was quiet. Not many tourists. Wrong time of year, and a weekday. Actually, it was quite nice at first. Dad's mood was pretty good and he was joking with me, talking about the future and how he was going to try to improve things. He always said things like that but he had a way of making it sound like it was the first time he'd said it, and he could make you believe it. I wanted to believe it. The weather was nice at first and I was enjoying being outside. And then the weather changed, and the clouds rolled in and suddenly we were surrounded by mist and wet.

Sound of rainfall and the rear of the stage starts to fill with smoke/mist. ROB and DANIELLE are walking across the front of the stage as the smoke thickens when VERY SUDDENLY the GHOST appears from the mist and tried to grab DANIELLE who is to the rear. DANIELLE sees it and screams, stepping forward and tripping, falling. The GHOST steps back into the mist but remain just visible on the stage.

ROB
(FS)

Danielle, are you okay?

DANIELLE screams again and starts crying. She points at the GHOST who is now simply standing in the mist, staring but radiating anger: clenched fists, shaking, etc. ROB stands and looks to where DANIELLE is pointing – he is almost nose to nose with the GHOST.

ROB
(FS)

Danny, for God's sake, there's fucking nothing here. Will you please stop it, you're spoiling things.

GHOST takes a step forward, so close to ROB that they're practically hugging and reaches either side of him to try and touch DANIELLE. She scuttles away, still crying.

DANIELLE

Dad please, make it go. Make it go away. Make her go away.

ROB

Make who go away? What? Oh for Christ's sake, Danny. Get up, girl. Let's go before the rain drowns us.

DANIELLE gets up. ROB and DANIELLE (still crying) carry on to the side of the stage where ROB leaves and DANIELLE returns to the apron and MURDOCH (calm by the time she gets there). The GHOST stands watching until she, too, steps back, exiting stage after the mist dissipates. Rainfall fades away.

DANIELLE

He couldn't see it. Not even when it was right there in front of him, the ghost of Charlotte. Not see or feel or sense it.

MURDOCH

You thought it was Charlotte?

DANIELLE

Yes. Who else could it have been?

MURDOCH

How could you tell?

DANIELLE

It…she was wet. I remembered what the man had said about her being thrown in the lake. And she wasn't in clothes, just some kind of sheet and the man had said her dress was found in the forest. It just made sense.

MURDOCH

Of course. What happened next?

DANIELLE

So we went back to the hotel and we did nothing much for
the rest of the day and things were quiet but every time I
tried to explain Dad'd cut me off, shut me up. And then…

She stops, upset.

MURDOCH

It's okay. Take your time. We can stop if you like?

DANIELLE

No, it's fine. It'll be fine. It's just hard. So, we were in the room
and I asked if we could go home because I wanted to see Mum.

ROB

(echoing, offstage)

No. Why would you want to go home? Don't be ungrateful,
Danny.

DANIELLE

So that was that, and Dad went for food but I didn't want
to go with him so he had something sent up from the
kitchen for me. I ate it and then was sitting waiting, not
really doing anything when—

*Sudden loud cracking sound, like wood splintering or
being hit hard, a fist hitting a door. DANIELLE doesn't
react because she's becoming hardened to it all now.*

DANIELLE

I could feel that I was being watched again, only this
time I could hear things as well. Footsteps in a forest,

water splashing and churning, branches breaking. Two people fighting but not saying anything, just grunting and panting. It got louder and louder until I felt like screaming for it to stop.

As she speaks those sounds start to play, rising in volume although never drowning DANIELLE out. She rises from her seat and starts to cross to the stage stairs. The noises carry on as she goes, with occasional choking sounds. On the opposite side of the stage ROB and the HOTELIER are seated across from each other, drinking. They make no noise.

As DANIELLE continues up onto and across the stage, she speaks and still the noises carry on.

DANIELLE
I had to get out. I wanted my dad! I couldn't walk fast, though I wanted to, but it was like there was some great weight dragging me, holding me back. I was so frightened I'd see her but I didn't, and everything moving at the corner of my eye was her, was Charlotte emerging from the shadows to snatch at me, poor Charlotte drowned in the lake, always cold and on the mezzanine her parents were staring at me from that painting, staring down, glaring as though they disapproved of everything and I wanted to cry but I couldn't and I wanted to scream but I couldn't and I wanted my dad, I wanted my mum, I wanted to *go home*.

This takes DANIELLE to the centre of the stage and the Roses' picture appears again, fading up. DANIELLE looks at it for a long moment and then carries on. The Roses fade away.

DANIELLE

I remember thinking that she must have been so happy when she met whoever she met. Maybe she thought he'd take her away, but he didn't, did he? He took her to the lake and… well… you know. So I carried on. I got across the foyer, all that dark wood and the rain beyond the windows making things grey and miserable.

The lights in the theatre start to ripple so that everywhere is bathed in shifting, moving shadows, like light reflecting off water.

DANIELLE

The hotel's bar was at the end of a corridor and it had a door with a window in it at the end and when I got there, I stopped, just watching my dad. I couldn't open the door. I just watched.

DANIELLE is still, watching ROB and the HOTELIER. They're sitting either side of a table/ bar drinking shots of whiskey, talking but silent. The GHOST shuffles onto the stage behind DANIELLE and comes to stand right behind her, very close. ROB and the HOTELIER suddenly let out peals of very male, very drunk laughter and throw down another whiskey each. From behind them a figure emerges. It's a POLICEMAN, who waits a moment then goes to stand besides ROB, putting a hand on his shoulder. ROB and the HOTELIER fall quiet.

DANIELLE
(FS)

I got it wrong, see. I was so wrong about it all. It was Dad. It was Dad. I wish I'd known, but I didn't, not 'til the very end.

The GHOST leans in and gently kisses DANIELLE'S cheek – on the scar it left – and then slips silently across the stage. Darkness falls. The sounds fade. Lights on the stage fade to almost nothing.

DANIELLE
(FS)

I wish I'd realised it was her, not Charlotte. I wish I'd known that the last time I felt my mother's touch would be a kiss in a hotel corridor from a ghost.

She steps off the stage.

MURDOCH
(now sitting very formally behind the desk)

The critical thing here is not the account of the haunting, it's the scar which has no reasonable explanation. A scar that two separate plastic surgeons have identified as the kind of scarring left after the subject has been in contact with something very cold. In effect, a frostbite scar.

COLLINS
(standing)

But surely there are other explanations for how Danielle got this scar, easier and based more in reality than Danielle being touched by a ghost? Surely, Mr Murdoch, you can't expect the jury to believe this is the afterlife?

MURDOCH

Not by itself, no. There's something else though. You've heard Danielle's description of the ghost, the one she gave to me: "Wrapped in white cloth, one eye showing, feet bare and dirty, wet"?

COLLINS

We all heard it, Mr Murdoch, what I'm trying to establish at this point is the relevance of any of this. Please, do enlighten us.

MURDOCH

I put in a Freedom of Information request for the crime scene photos still held by the police. Her father pled guilty to the murder of Danielle's mother so there was no trial, and neither this photo nor any other like it was ever made public. As can be seen from the photograph, Danielle's description of the ghost is exactly how her father left her mother, immersed in water, wrapped in white bedding but with one eye still uncovered.

A photo appears on the rear projection – a woman wrapped in a long white cloth, feet bare and muddy. Second photo appears, a close up of the GHOST face, eye showing. They are very similar (including cloth placement, etc,) but not quite identical. There is the sound of dripping water.

All lights snap out. Sound stops.

Scene III

Sound of a telephone. It rings several times and is then connected. A long pause.

MURDOCH

Hello?

MURDOCH

Hello? Is anyone there?

MEGAN

(*OS, voice distorted and 'telephony'*)

I have a story I can tell you. If you're interested, I mean?

Lights come up. The Apron is empty apart from a table. Throughout this entire scene and the next there is a constant sound of rain, not heavy or thundery but somehow dreary and dull. Ideally, the image of rainfall trickling down glass should be projected onto the rear of the stage for the entire time as well. The lighting should be subdued, muted. Very dull and dreary. There is a very low background murmur of voices, maybe a radio – general café noises.

MEGAN comes onto the apron, removes coat, etc, and sits at the table. A SERVER appears, goes to MEGAN, she orders and SERVER leaves.

MURDOCH appears on the stage, crossing it quickly, hunched against the rain. He has on a coat and is carrying a satchel. He descends the steps, checks something on his phone and then steps onto the apron. He sees MEGAN, walks over to her.

MURDOCH

Is it Megan?

MEGAN

Yes. You're Richard? Mr Murdoch?

MURDOCH

Richard is fine, thank you, and yes I am. May I?

MEGAN

Of course.

He takes his coat off and sits

MURDOCH

I'm sorry, have you been here long? The weather slowed me down.

MEGAN

Me too, so no, don't worry. I'd literally just sat down. This is a lovely cafe isn't it? Do me a favour, before we start, look around at it, listen to it. Get its vibe. Try to remember how it feels.

MURDOCH looks around, confused but doing as he's told. As he does, the very low sound of conversation and background music, lighter than the rain, fills the air. It lasts for the next few minutes, slowly fading as MEGAN starts her story.

MURDOCH

I'm not sure that I understand?

MEGAN

You will. Trust me.

MURDOCH

Okay. Of course.

MEGAN

I took the liberty of ordering for us, I hope that's okay?

SERVER brings a tray and places two tea pots, cups, milk jug, etc, on table.

MURDOCH

Perfect, you read my mind. So, you're still okay with going on the record and me recording your story? Using it in my work after?

MEGAN

Yes. I've nothing to hide and nothing to gain by telling you. I just need to tell it.

MURDOCH

Well then. When you're ready, please begin.

Scene IV – The Elms, Morecambe

MEGAN

I asked to meet you here, Mr Murdoch—

MURDOCH

Richard

MEGAN

Sorry, Richard. I asked to meet you here, Richard, because it's very close to where the story I'm going to tell you happened. It was down the road from here in a hotel called The Elms. It was lovely there, good roast dinners on a Sunday, good views over the bay and out to sea, reasonable prices and the kind of old-fashioned style you don't get in modern places.

Photos of The Elms/seaside hotels appear on rear of stage, fading in then out. The photos are all old, B&W, and include party scenes, etc.

MEGAN

My husband Tom, God Rest him, and I moved here not long after we were married and we raised out child here. We were happy. Life was good. This is a good place to raise children. There's the beach, the sea for swimming when it wasn't being filled with sewage. It was nice.

MURDOCH

It sounds like it.

MEGAN

So when our daughter Charlie announced she was engaged, we were happy. The Elms felt like a natural place to have the wedding breakfast and reception. Lots of good memories for us there, lots of rooms, reasonable prices and a free carpark. That's important, isn't it? You're asking people to come and celebrate with you so you don't want them to spend a lot, do you?

MURDOCH

I'd assume not. I'm not married but I understand what you mean.

MEGAN

It's a shame you're not. Married, I mean. Marriage, being with someone, it's a good way to be in the world. You can hold each other up and help each other on.

MURDOCH

Yes. I was due to be married but she died.

MEGAN

Oh, I'm so sorry.

MURDOCH

It was a few years ago now, but thank you. So, the Elms…?

MEGAN

Sorry, yes. We started to get everything ready, were planning and booking and organising but then Tom, my husband, he died suddenly. He was about to retire, we had such plans, but he had a heart attack and he was gone. I came home to find him in his chair, the television on and a drink on the table next to him. He died with a smile on his face, at least. That's something, isn't it?

MURDOCH

Yes.

Pictures appear on rear stage: a coffin in a grave, a group of mourners around an open grave, a distant skyline, empty buildings. There's a mournful air to them all.

MEGAN

My daughter, she wanted to put the wedding off, but I insisted we go ahead. It was a celebration of new life, after all, something bright in a world that felt like it had gone very dark. She agreed and we kept on preparing and I was enjoying it but my heart was broken. I felt like I'd lost a piece of myself.

MURDOCH

Yes. That's how it feels.

MEGAN

But was good to be busy. It didn't take away the sadness but some days I could cover it. If I felt overwhelmed I'd imagine Tom was there and I'd try to imagine the answer he'd give me if I asked, 'Tom, what do I do about this?'. It helped. You're wondering about the ghost, aren't you? Don't worry, I'm getting to her. One of the nice things about the Elms was they had a Master of Ceremonies who was so good at keeping things moving along. On the day of the wedding he took over from me and said

MEGAN rises as she speaks and walks up onto the stage, ending up next to where ARNOST appears.

ARNOST
(stepping out, FS, to Megan)

This is your day now, enjoy it. Be the mother of the bride, eat, drink, be merry, let me do the rest. [*To arriving guests*] Come in, come in! If you haven't been here before the cloakroom is there, the restrooms are there and the happy couple and wedding party are in the Bolland Suite just there. Follow the sound of people having fun!

Pop of champagne corks, lots of distant talk and occasional rounds of applause. There is a happy party going on somewhere close by. It's still raining.

ARNOST lifts a glass and a knife, taps repeatedly on the glass to get people's attention.

ARNOST
Ladies and gentlemen, the Mother of the Bride!

MEGAN
(From front of stage, holding cue cards with notes on)
I made a speech. I'd never done it before but I wanted to so that I could feel like Tom was part of the day. I used some notes I found that he'd made before he died.

MEGAN leaves the stage and returns to sit back in her chair opposite MURDOCH. Sudden blast of wedding first dance music. CHARLIE steps onto the apron, clearly having just come off the dance floor (slightly out of breath, she kisses MEGAN on the cheek).

CHARLIE
That was so lovely, what you said, Mum. Thank you for everything. For the day and the speech and the love and everything.

MEGAN
Ah, go away, you drunk thing, you'll make me cry. Honey, I'm tired and I'm missing your dad and I don't want to make everyone miserable with my silliness so I'm going to my room to rest. Have a lovely evening and I'll see you tomorrow.

CHARLIE

Oh, Mum, please stay! It's not silly, and people will understand.

MEGAN

No. It's for the best.

CHARLIE

You're sure?

MEGAN

Yes. Off you go now. Have fun.

MEGAN rises and walks up onto the stage, crosses it as the disco sounds fade, unlocks her door and enters her room. She starts to settle, (earrings out, shoes off, etc) when there is a knock at the door. Very loud.

MEGAN
(FS)

I thought it was maybe someone from the wedding party come to say goodnight, or to persuade me to come back down, but it wasn't.

Sudden blaze of spotlight, illuminating a girl, PEG. She is in an old-fashioned maid's outfit and has her hair down, head bowed.

PEG

Turn your sheets, ma'am?

MEGAN

Pardon?

PEG

Turn your sheets ma'am?

MEGAN
(FS)

Turn my sheets? Well, I suppose. Yes, that would be nice.

PEG comes in and starts turning the sheets back, plumping pillows, etc.

MEGAN
(FS but looking at Murdoch, sitting on the edge
of the stage, half ready for bed, hair down, etc)

I just thought it was some gimmick the hotel did, like Arnost being able to do the trick where you pour champagne into a glass and it froths up over the rim but doesn't spill, you know? Olde Worlde Charm sort of thing. Sending staff around in old uniforms to do these little tasks. How could I have known? Oh God, if I'd just said no, but I *couldn't*, when I opened the door she looked so sad and forlorn, so miserable. Saying no, it would have felt like kicking a puppy. God, I *wish* I'd kicked a puppy.

PEG finishes and goes to the door.

PEG

Your bed is ready for you. Is that all ma'am?

MEGAN

Yes, thank you. You've done an excellent job.

Lights fall.

MEGAN
(FS in darkness)

I went to bed. I wanted so much to talk to someone about the day but there was no one I could talk to. The person

I wanted to talk to about it all was Tom, of course, and he wasn't there. It was the first big family event we'd had without him, the first time I'd stayed in a hotel since he'd died, and all I could think was how happy he'd have been. The bed felt too large, the room was strange around me. I was awake for a long time before I fell asleep, and I didn't sleep well.

Sleeping sounds from the stage. A low light comes up slowly from on one side, just about illuminating PEG standing at the side of the stage, head down but clearly staring at where MEGAN is. She does not move. Scene holds for an uncomfortable length of time, until everyone is expecting something, anything to happen, but no…

Lights fade down.

Lights up. MEGAN is on stage with a group of people, all clearly saying goodbyes, hugs, etc. After they've gone she returns to the apron and sits with MURDOCH. Lights on stage fade.

MEGAN

I didn't notice anything wrong at first. I mean, I was a little sad the next day but I thought that was usual. I missed Tom, my daughter was married and left for her honeymoon and all I had to look forward to was going back to an empty house. Who wouldn't feel sad?

MURDOCH

There's a year of firsts, isn't there? All the things you do for the first time without them. It's hard. Their birthday, your birthday, Christmas, holiday, all those things that we share without realising it.

MEGAN

Yes. So, anyway, I went home, and everything was low and grey and *I* was low and grey and I thought, well, it'll get better. But it didn't. Not when I got a lovely letter from Charlie, not when I read the messages that people sent me. I thought it was normal to keep feeling like this. I didn't know until a couple of weeks later that it wasn't me.

MEGAN gets up and goes to the stage, lies on it then sits up. Stage remains dark.

MEGAN
(FS)

I woke one night because I was sure someone was in the room with me, was *sure* of it. I could feel them, feel them watching me, staring at me.

Very bright spot snaps on. PEG is standing as close to MEGAN as she can be without being seen before the spotlight! MEGAN screams, rolls off stage and back onto apron. Light snaps off. PEG exits.

MEGAN

She was in the room with me. I saw her, clear as I'm seeing you now.

MURDOCH

Let me play devil's advocate, just for a moment. Could it have been a dream? Some flashbulb in your sleeping brain that woke you? Have you ever done that jerking thing as you fall asleep that wakes you up? Sometimes it comes along with hallucinations.

MEGAN

I wondered that too but then I was fully awake so it doesn't explain what happened next.

PEG appears to left of Apron and walks towards MEGAN. Her head is down, she is not threatening in any way.er hands are ehld out azs though asked for them to be held MEGAN makes a series of choked 'no, no' sounds and backs away, stumbling up the steps where she crosses, panicking, to the other side, followed by PEG. PEG stops at centre stage as MEGAN returns to the table with MURDOCH.

MEGAN

She was there, and then she wasn't. It wasn't a panic attack or a hallucination, she was there. I heard her feet on the floor, saw her as clearly as I'm seeing you. I spent the rest of the night awake. And thinking about our first meeting, about what had happened.

MURDOCH

Did you not think she was simply a disturbed person, or that she'd broken in?

MEGAN

No. There was a feeling to her, looking at her made me as sad as I'd ever been, an overwhelming sadness, worse that when Tom had died. It wasn't human. That something so sad had chosen to visit me was terrible because I didn't know why. Didn't, until I realised what I'd done.

MURDOCH

What you'd done?

MEGAN

What I'd done. I'd shown her some kindness, you see. I'd let her in.

MURDOCH
I don't quite understand.

MEGAN
Neither did I, not then, but I do now. I let that sad, dead little thing into my room, I invited her in, and she came and she simply didn't go. Once I'd calmed that night, I tried to persuade myself if was a dream, just like you said, but I started to see her again and again, and not just in the bedroom.

MEGAN gets up and starts walking around the theatre, in amongst the audience. PEG follows, only moving when MEGAN is not looking at her, always still when she looks over at her. Peg shouldn't move like a ghost but like a servant – quiet, unobtrusive mist occasionally drifting from her. PEG never tries to hide from MEGAN, she simply lowers her head and stands still when MEGAN looks directly at her.

MEGAN
(as she moves around)
I'd be in the shop and see her at the end of the aisle, just watching me. I'd be in a café with a friend and she'd be stood in amongst the tables. I went to the theatre and she was stood at the back of the circle, just at the edge of the seats, always looking at me, never at the stage or what was happening around her.

MEGAN moves up onto stage. Moving pictures start to play across her. PEG follows, standing close to her shoulder.

MEGAN
(FS)
When I watched TV at night she'd be in the corner of the room, caught in the shadows.

Lights click out.

MEGAN
(FS)

And she was always, always in my room at night. Standing in the corner, head down, never approaching me, just... there. Always there.

MEGAN moves back down to the apron and sits again. PEG goes offstage.

As MEGAN says this next section a baby starts crying, not loud but enough to hear, and continues until the end of this piece.

MEGAN

And that's not the worst of it, not really. It was scary at first, then annoying and eventually it was just like a habit, something I'd forget until I'd see her and be startled. It's hard to believe isn't it? That we can get used to something like that but we can, Mr... Richard. We can.

MURDOCH

Yes.

MEGAN

The worst of it was the sadness. Whoever she was, she was such a sad thing and her sadness was like a cloud, like a contagion. Everywhere I went, after a while, the mood would start to fall. I'd see people around me start to lose whatever energy and happiness they'd had in them when I came in. When I came in with her. Something awful must have happened to her in her life, to be so sad, to be so miserable and lost, because that's how people ended up feeling around her, miserable and lost and hopeless. It got so I stopped going places, I just stayed at home and hoped she'd eventually find someone else whose bed needed turning and that when she'd done that, she'd finally leave me alone.

MURDOCH
That must have been hard.

MEGAN
Oddly, no. I'd been sad anyway because of Tom, so carrying this new sadness felt like just another part of the same thing. People assumed I didn't want to go out because I was struggling with my grief and I let them think that. It was easier all around.

COLLINS, TIDYMAN and MYERS come onto the stage. MURDOCH straightens, turns his attention to them. MEGAN moves slightly back from the table and out of the 'attention zone'.

COLLINS
(FS)
Mr Murdoch, please tell me that your 'proof' isn't simply the retelling of a story you were told in a café one rainy day?

MURDOCH
Of course not. What Megan told me is a story, yes, but it's one that can be at least partially verified.

COLLINS
(FS)
And I assume you've done that? And you'll enlighten the court?

TIDYMAN
(FS)

Your honour…

MYERS
(FS)

Agreed. Mr Collins, please try to keep the sarcasm to a minimum.

COLLINS
(FS)

Your honour. As I was saying, can you present the court with this verification?

MURDOCH

Yes. We went back through the hotel records for the past five years and emailed and wrote to every person listed that we had contact details for. We asked if they'd had any odd experiences in the hotel but we didn't mention chambermaids or sheets so as not to bias things. We just asked.

COLLINS
(FS)

And the results were…?

MURDOCH

Most people didn't respond, of course, and quite a few had changed addresses so never got the original messages, but we did get back eleven separate responses listing strange experiences in the hotel.

COLLINS
(FS)

'Strange experiences'? That's hardly proof of anything, is it?

MURDOCH

Decide for yourself. Two of them had no common elements with Megan's story, but eight of those people reported a maid coming to their room very late at night, being dressed in old-fashioned clothes and having an air of sadness to her, offering to turn their sheets down. Eight strangers reporting the same thing, months and sometimes years apart.

COLLINS
(FS)

Well…

MURDOCH

All eight told us that they turned the girl away.

COLLINS
(FS)

It's hardly cast-iron, is it, Mr Murdoch?

MURDOCH

A ninth reply came not from a former guest but from his son. After staying at the Elms his father, he reported, had told the story of a sad little girl who came to his room at the hotel with an offer to turn his sheets down. He'd accepted.

COLLINS
(FS)

AH! So you've spoken to him, then? The father? He's your proof?

MURDOCH

No. We can't. His son told us that he'd killed himself three weeks after his stay at the Elms.

Attention back to MEGAN now. COLLINS and the others exit.

MEGAN

Besides, I thought that eventually she'd stop. That her spirit or whatever it was would go back to the Elms. I used to dream about her, leaving me at night and going back there, walking along the corridors knocking on doors and saying, 'Turn your sheets, ma'am' or 'Turn your sheets, sir' to anyone who answered and I thought, well, one day someone will say yes. And when they do, she'll go and follow them. Haunt them, I suppose.

MURDOCH

Yes. That might make sense. And all this happened when?

MEGAN

Nearly two years ago.

MURDOCH

So how long did she stay with you?

MEGAN
(laughs sadly)

About 4 weeks after Charlie's wedding, the Elms closed unexpectedly. Apparently it had been losing money for years and the decision was made to sell it. Within two months the building had been demolished and an office block was being built in its place.

MURDOCH

So what…

MEGAN

Do you remember me asking you to have a look around this café, to take in its atmosphere? Do the same again now. Hasn't it changed? (*Sound of baby crying gets a little louder during this section*) Hasn't it become sad? She's still here, Richard, she's *still with me*. She's standing in the corner of the café right now.

Lights come up during the last speech and illuminate PEG right rear of stage, still standing head down and face out of view. Mist drifts from her occasionally.

MURDOCH starts to turn and MEGAN leans over the table like a snake, very fast, grabs him, grips him tight and holds his attention to her. She may grab his face so that he can't physically turn his head.

MEGAN

NO! Don't look at her. If you do she might start after you, and I can't have that. She's been mine for nearly two years, my burden, and I'll take her with me.

MURDOCH

But you'll—

MEGAN

No. That's the way it's got to be. She's always been so sad, you see, and this may be her chance. When I die, maybe she'll be free. No Elms. No sheets to turn. No more misery to inflict. It's not her fault, whatever happened to her to make her this way wasn't her fault, so maybe I can carry her with me until we're both released. I'm choosing this, do you understand? She's mine, and I'll take care of her. Do not look around, Richard. Please.

MEGAN rises and walks to the side of the stage as the noise of rain and the baby crying increases. She leaves without looking back. PEG follows.

With a last cry, baby falls into silence.

Lights down.

ACT II
Scene I

MYERS is seated, TIDYMAN, COLLINS and MURDOCH are in front of her.

TIDYMAN
It's not like it's not got precedents. It's not even that unusual.

MYERS
Are you really lecturing me on the application of the law within the court system, Mr Tidyman? Really?

TIDYMAN
No, your honour, of course not. I'm merely—

MYERS
You're merely lecturing me on the application of the law within the court system. Mr Collins, I assume you're against this plan?

COLLINS
Of course. It's nonsense.

TIDYMAN
It's not nonsense.

MYERS
That's to be decided. Mr Murdoch, if you'd like to explain it to me again. Slowly and carefully, if you please. Pretend I'm a beginner in all this. An idiot, if you will.

MURDOCH
I don't think that I'll do that, your honour, but I will try to set out what we're proposing and hoping to achieve.

MYERS

A sensible approach.

As MURDOCH says the next, film of a bleak, windswept landscape plays across the stage. No sounds though.

MURDOCH

The defence in this case is that the accused was scared by unexplained phenomena which led to the death, yes? Well, what we propose is to see if the jury experience any of the same responses as the accused. We take the jury to three different farms, including the site of the death. They aren't told which farm is which and they're taken before they hear the defence testimony so that there's no risk of confirmation bias, no chance of them being pre-empted to experience anything.

COLLINS

This is preposterous. Are we seriously considering this?

MYERS

We might be. Mr Murdoch?

MURDOCH

At each farm, individuals are given a map with places indicated and times for them to be in each room. They're told to be in the places at the time and to simply stand for five minutes, recording anything they see, hear, feel, anything at all, in notebooks. They also keep a record of any noises they themselves make those times so that if, say, they sneeze and other people report hearing a sneeze we can rule it out. They're told not to talk to each other about their experiences in those times. We also take various visual and audio recordings of the site so that we have a reference that we can go to for external corroboration. Then, after we collate the various notes, we can see if there are any commonalities.

COLLINS

Commonalities? Are you serious?

MYERS

It does seem a little… loose, Mr Murdoch.

MURDOCH

Well, it's not exactly scientific, I grant you, because it's not lab conditions but just imagine: say all the jurors report nothing in any of the bedrooms we ask them to go to except for one, and in that one four or five report a feeling of sadness. If that's similar to what the defendant says he felt in that room then there's some backup for what he's saying. It would mean he's maybe telling the truth.

TIDYMAN

And bear in mind, your honour, that my client isn't claiming to be innocent of the crime, only that there are extenuating circumstances. This is simply a chance to see if those claims have any kind of veracity.

COLLINS

It won't prove anything! It's all absolute crap!

MYERS

Mr Collins.

COLLINS

I apologise but—

MYERS

Mr Tidyman, I assume that you and Mr Murdoch will be there?

TIDYMAN

Of course. In a supervisory capacity and to explain the process, answer questions, but not to get involved in any other way.

MYERS

So as to avoid contamination?

TIDYMAN

Yes.

MYERS

And the other two farms, they're ready to go?

MURDOCH

Everything's sorted. I didn't want there to be any delays if we got the go-ahead. We've found two farms of a similar age and construction but which have no recorded history of hauntings. We've agreements in place with the farmers to have access to each for a three hour block, which is enough time to get the jurors in and out without any stress.

MYERS

And your efficiency is appreciated. Mr Collins, your strenuous objections have been noted but it occurs to me that if we are allowing the defence to bring Mr Murdoch to the stand, then we should trust Mr Murdoch's actions in support of his testimony. Juror visits aren't common but they have, as Mr Tidyman rightly says, many precedents. So we'll go ahead, but I expect all the information gathered to be shared, whether it supports the defendant's case or not, you understand?

TIDYMAN
Of course. Many thanks, your honour.

MYERS
Don't thank me. Farms are muddy, stinking places and you're going to three of them.

Film of landscape blurs, fades and finally vanishes.

Scene II

All from stage

JURORS 1 and 2 enter from the side. Both are holding large printed plans – building layouts – and pads/clipboards and pencils.

JUROR 1
I'm terrible with maps and plans. Where are we?

JUROR 2
Hold on. We're in the farmhouse, yes? So I think that the two rooms ahead are where we need to be. What time is it?

JUROR 1
Five to. Do you know what we're doing here?

JUROR 2
Checking the rooms I think.

JUROR 1
No, I mean at all the farms. I never thought jury duty would mean walking round shitty places like this, did you?

JUROR 2
Nope.

JUROR 1
Does this count as 'talking about it', do you think?

JUROR 2
No, I don't think so. I think they just meant don't talk about the case, and what we hear or whatever in the rooms. It's about time, we should get in.

FS JURORS 1 and 2 go to separate parts of the stage, JUROR 2 passing through a connecting door to get there. Both stand in the centre of their halves and wait, in attentive 'I am concentrating' poses. JUROR 1 retains this pose thoughout the entire next section, occasionally fidgeting, but never reacting. They hear/experience nothing.

There is a long moment of silent which gets to be just about uncomfortable and then there's a gentle tapping. JUROR 2 looks around, it stops, they shrug and makes a note, checking the time to record it properly.

There are a series of knocks, louder than the tapping, more rapid. JUROR 2 checks time, notes again. JUROR 2 yawns, grins, notes it in case someone else heard it.

Long silence. Both JUROR 1 and JUROR 2 fidget a little.

There is a sudden, very loud crash (wood against wood). JUROR 2 jumps along with audience, drops their notebook. They take a moment and bend to pick it up and there's another loud crash. This time JUROR 2 shrieks a little, then laughs at their nerviness. They pick up the notebook, make another note and then shrieks again as there is a long, drawn-out screech, wet wood splintering or tearing.

As the noise drops, another takes its place – a long, low wail or groan. There are no words in it, it may not even be human, and it rises in volume and pitch.

JUROR 2

What is this? Who's there? This isn't funny.

The noise responds by turning into a long series of scratches and associated noises which ends in a hoarse groan.

JUROR 2

Now look…

Another set of noises, very sudden, gibbering and shrieking and animal grunts and growls. JUROR 2 backs away, reaching the centre of the stage and tries to open the connecting door between the room and where JUROR 1 is.

The door does not open.

JUROR 2 shakes it but it still doesn't open. The noises pause.

JUROR 2

Hey! Hey, please, the door won't open. Help!

JUROR 1 does not respond. JUROR 2 starts banging on the door.

JUROR 2

Hey! Hey, please!

The noises resume, even louder. There's a pause.

JUROR 2

Please, stop. Whoever this is, please stop.

Tries the door again. It still won't open. JUROR 2 is getting more and more frantic as the noise mutates, becoming almost like a static swirl with almost-voices in it.

JUROR 2 backs away from the door, trips and falls back, ends up scrambling backwards. The lights all drop except for a spotlight on JUROR 2, a narrow point. The noises carry on, but from JUROR 2's reaction they're moving around. They swing out as though to ward away things in the air. They are crying now, screaming as things appear to attack.

There is a piercing scream, not from JUROR 2. Another.

There is a rushing sound, a whirling wind but that moves nothing. All through this JUROR 2 is moving away, crawling around the back of the stage, alternately trying to escape it or punching out at things the audience cannot see.

JUROR 2
Get away! Get away! Leave me alone!

The noises change again, warping down to become a dark, hoarse voice that lets out a ragged chuckle that finally tails off to nothing.

JUROR 2
Please…

Another crash.

All this has taken approximately 5 minutes. The lights on the stage come up. JUROR 1 looks at their watch, sticks the notebook in their pocket and goes to the door. They try to open door but it won't open. They try harder. Nothing.

JUROR 1
Hello? The door's stuck.

JUROR 2
(very quiet, weak)

Help. Please help.

JUROR 1

What? Are you okay?

JUROR 2
(screams weakly)

JUROR 1 rattles at the door, then kicks it open. Sees JUROR 2 on the floor and rushes to them.

JUROR 1

What happened?

JUROR 2
(screams again, stronger this time)

JUROR 1

For God's sake, what happened?

JUROR 2

Please, has it stopped? Make it stop.

JUROR 1

Make what stop? There's nothing here.

JUROR 2

There was. There was. Take me out of here. Please.

They stand and leave the stage.

Lights down.

Scene III

MURDOCH and TIDYMAN are in casual clothes, leaning against the stage. They have coats on. The atmosphere is relaxed. Tidyman has a flask in her hand.

TIDYMAN

I wonder if this'll work.

MURDOCH

The trips or the defence in general?

TIDYMAN

Either. Both.

MURDOCH

I suppose it depends on whether today yields results. Frankly, I'm amazed Myers has let me anywhere near the defence at all, so every step from there is a victory of sorts.

TIDYMAN

I suppose so, yes. I'm not sure we're making legal history but we might be setting a series of strange precedents. Does that look like rain to you?

MURDOCH

Yes. Did you hear that?

TIDYMAN

No, what?

MURDOCH

A scream. I think it was a scream.

TIDYMAN

Shit. Do you think someone's in trouble?

MURDOCH

Maybe. Or they've seen a ghost.

TIDYMAN

That'd be something! Should we go and find them?

MURDOCH

No, we'd mess up the experiment. We can't be involved, remember? They know to meet us here at the cow shed when they're done, they'll all be here soon. They know they can leave any of the designated waiting spots early if they aren't comfortable. Oh good, here's the rain.

TIDYMAN

Damnation! Help me get this door open, we'll wait inside.

They leave.

Scene IV

All from stage

JUROR 3 walks onto the stage – she is also holding a plan, notebook, etc. She stops left-stage. She is bright, cheery, breezy. Everything seems fun to them.

JUROR 3
(to herself)
'Walkway 2'. Do we think that's this one then?

She plays with the plan, then looks at her watch.

JUROR 3
Best guess is, it is. So I have to stand here and listen for 5 minutes, in… *(looks at watch)* just under two minutes. Just on time. Come on jury duty, they said. It'll be fun, they said. You'll get to stand in a set of godforsaken farms and listen for God knows what, they said. Well, they didn't. I wish they had, I'd have found some excuse to get out of it all. Oh, wait, time's a-getting, best be listening now. Is it time? No. Maybe we should get acquainted, Walkway Number two? I'm Jerry, Jerry the Juror, and I've got to listen to you for five minutes in… one minute. I'm sure you're a lovely walkway but you look a bit cold and miserable to me. Perhaps you need cheering up? I could tell you a joke? No? Okay. No jokes. No, I have no idea why we're doing this, they wouldn't tell us, but thank you for asking. If you find out from anyone else, will you let me know? No? Jeez, you're hard to please. You're not as much fun as the other rooms I've had to stand in today. Ah ha! Look at that! It's pretty much time now so I'll be going quiet and listening. See you on the other side!

J3 falls silent, concentrating.

The theatre lights dim slightly as clouds roll in – except for a single rear projection on the right hand of the stage – a thing that might be a tree in silhouette, or a thin cowled figure. It is motionless.

JUROR 3 looks around, still obviously concentrating. Sees the tree figure, makes a note in their pad but also on the plan, clearly trying to work out where the tree-figure is located for accurate reporting.

JUROR 3 moves around a little, looking at other things. When they look back, has the figure increased in size, come a little closer? Just a little? Now it appears to be moving, just a little, fluttering. Could still be a tree, of course, waving in the wind.

JUROR 3 takes several steps towards the figure, trying to make it out more clearly. As they step the figure increases in size as the distance between them closes. Now other things are coming into view – a wall and a five-bar gate at the figure's side. If they're 'normal' size then the figure is very tall – perhaps 7 feet – and thin, a cowled shape that might be a monk. It is entirely black, no details are visible, and still its edges flutter. It looks like it might be a monk… or maybe the grim reaper without a scythe.

JUROR 3 makes another note on their pad. To do so, they look down, and when they look up the figure is larger, closer. It raises what might be an arm, pointing in the direction of JUROR 3. It is still entirely black, a shadow

JUROR 3 steps back, makes a startled noise – the figure does not shrink at all. Confused, JUROR 3 makes a quick note of the noise they made and the time.

There is another slight darkening of the theatre lights and then the rain starts. The sound of rain – not heavy but constant, dreary. The figure doesn't respond to it at all, just carries on fluttering and being otherwise motionless but JUROR 3 says "SHIT" and gets in a mess zipping up her coat and then noting again her noise-making in their pad. By the time she's finished, the figure has faded to nothing.

A shadow crosses the stage. It might be the figure, but it might not. As the shadow passes over JUROR 3 they shiver. The shadow stretches and drifts over the audience, moves back and fades. JUROR 3 watches, confused.

JUROR 3

What the crap?

Checks watch, makes a note

JUROR 3

Time's up so I can make noises again, thank God.

Notices that figure is gone.

JUROR 3

What the good god damn? Hey! HEY! Is there someone there?

Looks around.

JUROR 3

No. No, of course there isn't you idiot. It was someone messing about, or it's some trick that they're playing as part of the defence. Sod it. I've made my notes, they can have them.

JUROR 3 leaves and the stage lights drop to nothing. A very tall, thin cowled figure steps onto stage, watching JUROR 3 leaving, then slides back off without turning.

Scene V

*MURDOCH and TIDYMAN enter, shaking off rain,
stopping in the centre of the apron.*

TIDYMAN

Jesus, it stinks.

MURDOCH

It's a cowshed, of course it stinks.

As if in agreement, a cow makes a lowing moo.

MURDOCH

Haven't you been to a farm before?

TIDYMAN

God, no. Why would I have wanted to do that?

MURDOCH

You don't have kids? Taken them to a petting farm or
anything like that?

TIDYMAN

I've got kids but the closest they get to nature is playing
football on the field at the weekend or going on the beach
in summer. We're townies.

MURDOCH

Me too, but I had a fiancée who was a country girl and kept
dragging me out of the city at the weekends. Apparently it
was good for me.

TIDYMAN

'Had'?

MURDOCH

She… she died.

TIDYMAN

I'm sorry, I didn't mean—

MURDOCH

It's okay. It was a few years back. I'm not over it, not exactly, but I can talk about her now without it hurting too much. Life goes on, doesn't it?

Another cow lows. A second returns its call. There is the metallic ring of hooves hitting a gate or pen side. The two of them stand in the middle, waiting, until TIDYMAN speaks.

TIDYMAN

It's not easy though.

MURDOCH

No.

TIDYMAN

Can I ask, is that—

MURDOCH

No, it's not why I started in parapsychology. It's not why I hunt ghosts. I was doing this work anyway. And no, I'm not hoping to do enough of this work so that I learn how to raise her ghost and get some kind of closure. You don't need to worry, Mr Tidyman, I won't start crying about her in the witness stand. You can rely on me.

Collins comes into the cowshed.

COLLINS

Crying about who?

TIDYMAN

Nothing and no one, Jim. You're happy with how this has all been carried out?

COLLINS

Happy might be pushing it a bit but I'll accept that the way the day has run has been within the parameters we agreed with Judge Myers. It's nice to get a day out from the office. Shame it's not anywhere nicer, though. You should try harder, Alice. Poor show. Hey, did you hear a scream before?

MURDOCH

I thought I did. Ms Tidyman—

TIDYMAN

Alice, please.

MURDOCH

Alice didn't. If any of the jurors heard it or made it, it should be in the notes.

Muted cow sounds, shuffling and clanks. Nothing serious or sinister, just farm animal noises.

COLLINS

I still think this is nonsense, you know. What's this going to prove? It's nonsense.

TIDYMAN

We know, Jim, we know.

COLLINS

How many more stops have the poor buggers got to make? It's getting cold and this isn't exactly a friendly place, is it?

MURDOCH

It's not great, no. And there's just one. They should start arriving here in about 10 minutes or so. I'll collect the notebooks and—

COLLINS

I'd prefer to be present when that happens.

TIDYMAN

Jim's right. We should all be present so that there can be no question of tampering by any of us raised later.

MURDOCH

That's a good point. We should also get the jurors to sign each page at the bottom of their notes so that there's no chance of things being added later. Jim, if it's okay to call you that, you should be with us to collect the recording equipment as well.

COLLINS

Yes. Right, I'll go back to the coach, make sure the driver's ready for us. Get the heaters on.

TIDYMAN

Okay. I'll wait with Mr Murdoch—

MURDOCH

Richard

TIDYMAN

I'll wait with Richard for the jurors and we'll bring them back as a group.

COLLINS

Good. I'll see you there.

Collins leaves. The cows make louder noises.

TIDYMAN

Well, we—

There's a very loud clang as of a barn door being kicked open or pushed so hard it bangs against the wall and JURORS 1 & 2 walk in, JUROR 2 clearly still upset.

TIDYMAN

You nearly gave me a heart attack! You're the first here, so… what… hey, wait, are you okay?

JUROR 1

No, he's had a fright and—

MURDOCH

Don't tell us! That's the whole point. Is it written down? With timings?

JUROR 1

I don't think you understand, he was nigh-on hysterical when I found him.

TIDYMAN

Hysterical?

JUROR 2
(collapsing to a kneeling position)
Get me out of here.

MURDOCH goes and stands in front of JUROR 2.

MURDOCH

It's okay. Whatever it was, it's fine now. You're here, away
from it.

*JUROR 2 looks up at MURDOCH and then, suddenly,
screams.*

Lights down.

Scene VI

There's a table on the stage with an old fashioned radio on it but nothing else.

JURORS 4 and 5 walk onstage.

JUROR 4
So this is the dining room?

JUROR 5
Think so. Hold on, let me check.

Plays with plan, nodding

JUROR 5
Yes, this is the dining room.

JUROR 4
Is this one of the ones we're supposed to stop in?

JUROR 5
No, not here.

The radio lights come on. JURORS do not notice.

JUROR 4
So where are we supposed to be next? How many more have we got to do?

JUROR 5
One each. I don't know about you but I've to do the... erm... front lounge.

JUROR 4

Wait, I'll check my list.

JUROR 4 checks their sheet.

JUROR 4

Ah, yeah, the hallway is the one place I've not done. It's like Cluedo isn't it? I keep expecting to find a body and a lead pipe.

JUROR 5

It was Colonel Mustard in the Scullery with the rope.

JUROR 4

This place has a scullery?

JUROR 5

Yes, Colonel Mustard has just killed someone in it.

JUROR 4

Well, it the right kind of place to have a scullery, isn't it? Actually, it's the right kind of place for a murder too. It's so, I don't know, so *grim*. I know farmers are vital for the economy and all that, but God, I wouldn't want to live somewhere like this. Would you?

Very softly at first, almost inaudible, but getting louder until it's not too hard to make out, an old song starts playing. It's mournful, a 1920s sort of thing, with a female vocalist. It's very crackly and static-y, like an old radio broadcast.

JUROR 5

Christ no. Can you imagine, waking up every day at the crack of dawn and seeing all the mud and crap? I'd go mad. You're right, it's certainly run down and old. All three of the farms they've had us at today have been old and worn, haven't they?

JUROR 4

They have. Why three farms, do you think?

JUROR 5

Don't know. Ours is, as they say, not to reason why.

JUROR 4

So we just do and die?

JUROR 5

Well... hopefully not. I'd quite like to go home after all this is over. I'd not planned on dying yet. There's stuff I want to do. Pizzas I've not eaten, films I've not seen, places I want to go to, that kind of thing.

JUROR 4

Ha, I get you. Maybe let's not die then? Hey, what's that? Is that music?

JUROR 5

It is. Where's it... hold on, the radio's on.

JUROR 4

So it is.

JUROR 4 goes to the radio, examines it. The music gets louder, not uncomfortable yet but approaching that level. JURORS 4 and 5 have to raise their voices to speak to each other.

JUROR 4

How?

JUROR 5

How what?

JUROR 4

How is it on?

JUROR 4 holds up the radio's cord. It's frayed and there's no plug.

JUROR 5

Is it battery powered? I mean, it's got to be getting power from somewhere?

JUROR 4 turns the radio round, examining it. When they look back up at JUROR 5, their face tells us what we already suspect: the radio isn't battery powered.

JUROR 4

It's—

Huge burst of static and feedback, very loud. JUROR 4 drops the radio back onto the table. The static squall stops and the song resumes but slower now, slightly distorted, and much louder, almost painfully so.

JUROR 5

What's going on?

JUROR 4

How the Hell should I know?

JUROR 5

It's a trick, right?

JUROR 4

Must be. Strange one, though. I mean, what's the point of it? Are they trying to scare us?

The song starts slowing and speeding up now, the sound warping.

JUROR 5

Well, what do we do?

JUROR 4

Why are you asking me? I haven't got a damn clue! No one gave me any instructions about what to do when a radio with no obvious power source starts playing by itself! Unless they gave you any kind of guidance for this situation, the best I can think of is, let's get out of here.

JUROR 5

To where?

JUROR 4

Anywhere.

The music shifts, becomes a long low stretching voice. It's impossible to make out words but it might be a chant or a ritual.

JUROR 5

To the last places?

JUROR 4

Christ no. I'm done with this. I'm going to the rendezvous point.

The voice starts merging back into the song. It is still slow, distorting. It sounds like a record where the turntable is being slowed and then let free again. As it plays, it now starts to quieten.

JUROR 5

That's a plan I can get behind. Let's go.

JUROR 4

Yeah. I've had it with farms and mud and cold bloody rooms for today.

They leave. The radio lights flare very brightly for a moment then fade down again.

The song, now playing at its usual speed, fades and the stage lights drop to blackness. Only the radio is emitting light, still lying on the table. The song comes to an end. The radio sits, still lit, for 10 or so seconds and then it, too, clicks off.

Scene VII

JUROR 2 is sitting on the edge of the stage, JUROR 1 stood next to them. MURDOCH and TIDYMAN are standing a little away from them initially talking in hushed whispers.

TIDYMAN

This isn't good, Richard. The poor thing's practically traumatised. We need to get everyone out of here.

MURDOCH

I agree. Do you want to take these two to the coach while I wait for the rest of them?

TIDYMAN

Yes. We took everyone's phones, didn't we? I wish we hadn't, we could have texted them all to tell them to come back.

Cow moos, kicks stall, etc. Louder than before.

MURDOCH

I know. I have the master list of who should be where and when in the house and grounds so if they don't get here soon I'll go and fetch them. Hopefully no one else has had anything similar happen to them.

TIDYMAN

That's the problem, isn't it? I mean, what did happen?

MURDOCH

I don't know. Hopefully they'll calm down enough to tell us. Maybe it'll help with the defence.

TIDYMAN

Maybe. Or Maybe Myers will have me struck off for petrifying a juror on a wild goose chase. I'm more worried about making sure they're okay.

MURDOCH

Who says it is? A wild good chase, I mean? But yes, you're right, we need to make sure they're okay before we start looking at anything else.

JUROR 3 enters the cowshed. They don't seem particularly bothered by their experience and are still talking to themselves.

JUROR 3

Well, this is a lovely place, isn't it? Cow shit and mud and rain. It's like a holiday in Sedbergh[1]. Any tall spindly figures? No? Oh well, maybe at the next place. Oh, hello. I've done your experiment, do you want my notes? They're all here just like you wanted. I hope you can read my writing.

MURDOCH

Not yet, but thank you.

JUROR 2 moans slightly. Cows moo in reply.

MURDOCH

Alice, I think you should take the three of them. I'll wait here for the others.

JUROR 3

I must say I liked your little trick. Well done you!

---

1   Can be any town/area you hate.

JUROR 1

Trick?

JUROR 2

Not a trick. It wasn't a trick.

JUROR 1

What trick?

*Cows moo, etc. from this point the sound of cows mooing,
moving, banging into the sides of their stall is constant
behind the dialogue.*

JUROR 3

Yes, the—

MURDOCH
(interrupting)
Let's not talk about it, remember?

JUROR 3

Oh, yes, sorry.

JUROR 1

It was a sodding trick?

TIDYMAN

No, there are no tricks here today, not here or at the other
places. You have my word. Come on, let's get you all back
to the coach and the warm. I think we've still got coffee in
the flasks there and I think we could all do with something
to heat us up, couldn't we? Richard, you're okay to wait?

MURDOCH

I'm fine.

TIDYMAN

I'll get them settled and come back. I'm a little uneasy about this now, if I'm honest.

MURDOCH

Uneasy?

TIDYMAN

It's all beginning to feel a little out of control, don't you think? Tricks and whatever's happened to them?

MURDOCH

No. Damn. Maybe a little, yes. Damn, damn, damn.

TIDYMAN leads the others off the apron. MURDOCH settles back to wait.

Scene VIII

All from stage

JUROR 6 walks on – plan, pad, etc, all in hands. Stage is bare except for a table – no radio – and a chair. Stage rear has a projection of a window with rain running down the panes.

JUROR 6

So it's a kitchen. Oh good. Five minutes standing in a kitchen to add to the five minutes I've spent in a lounge, a muddy walkway, a bedroom and a hallway. Waste of bloody time it's been too.

JUROR 6 takes the chair and sets it at the side of the stage, sits on it. Sighing, they make a note of the time.

JUROR 6

Just in case anyone heard me moving the chair.

JUROR 6 looks at his watch again, sighs again, and then starts to do the concentrating pose the audience has become familiar with. Nothing happens. We hear rain and wind – distantly, not intrusive. It's almost reassuring, gently lulling us. JUROR 6 shuffles a little, getting comfortable on the seat. There is another wait right to the point the audience is starting to wonder if the actor has forgotten their lines. Actor playing role will need to judge this, and have a sign that the waiting period is over to start next section e.g. whistling.

FARMER walks onto the opposite side of the stage. They are in night clothes and a dressing gown.

FARMER
Who the hell are you? What are you doing here?

JUROR 6 is visible startled.

JUROR 6
I'm so sorry, they told us everything was empty, that everyone had gone. I'm—

FARMER
What the bloody hell do you think you're doing in my house?

JUROR 6
Please, let me explain, I'm here with the group from the court. From the trial? We're… well, I'm not sure exactly what we're doing but—

FARMER moves across the stage, reaching table.

FARMER
(*not quite looking directly at JUROR 6*)
Well, explain yourself! Do you think it's okay to just break in, to steal from hardworking people? Get yourself a proper job. Stop shrieking, damn you.

JUROR 6
Shrieking? No, I'm not, please, I'm sorry, this has all been a misunderstanding, if you'll just let me explain or go and get one of the organisers, they're waiting at the cowshed.

FARMER lunges as though to grab someone, reels back as if struck.

FARMER

What? Why, you little bastard!

FARMER comes again and this time appears to have been struck harder, spinning completely and falling to the floor on their hands and knees.

JUROR 6

What's going on? Are you okay?

FARMER starts to crawl away, jerks as though hit again and groans.

FARMER

I'll kill you, you little shit. I'll kill you.

FARMER jolts as though kicked in the stomach, rolls, carries on crawling for the side of the stage. JUROR 6 rises, dropping pad, etc, and moves to the centre of the stage.

FARMER

I'll kill you.

FARMER keeps crawling and jerking as though being hit and kicked. Whatever is happening is clearly a vicious attack. FARMER manages to reach the side of the stage and makes an effort, kicks back and then rises, first to their knees and then to a lurching stumble which takes them offstage.

JUROR 6

I don't—

FARMER shrieks offstage and there is a sound of a struggle – things breaking, etc – and then a another shriek and finally a shotgun blast, very loud, accompanied by the flash of a gunshot. FARMER's shrieks stop instantly, to be replaced by a terrible, wet, gurgling rasping that lasts for maybe three breaths before it, too, stops.

JUROR 6 walks to the table, suddenly becomes dizzy and has to grab it to stop themselves falling.

JUROR 6
What's going on? I don't understand.

The lights flicker and then dim.

JUROR 6
Now what? Please don't do this.

Although no one come onto the stage the FARMER's voice returns and repeats exactly the same phrases, noises, etc. Ends with another shotgun blast and flash of light.

JUROR 6 pushes themselves away from the table, falling to their knees and grabbing onto/hugging against the chair and starting to cry or groan.

JUROR 6
No no no, this isn't right, this is…

FARMER'S voice again, this time quieter and distorted as though being heard through a badly tuned radio. Shotgun blast, as light and bright as previous times.

Lights flicker, come back up. A shadow passes across the window at the rear of the stage.

JUROR 6 rises, still upset but trying to pull themselves together.

JUROR 6

What's happening? Please, someone, tell me.

The response is a distant knocking. JUROR 6 backs away from the stage side, focussing on where they entered the stage.

JUROR 6

What now? No more, please no.

MURDOCH walks onto the stage, looking around.

MURDOCH

Hello? Oh, there you are. I came to get you. Come on, we're leaving.

JUROR 6

Oh thank you. Thank you.

MURDOCH

Why? Shit, what's happened? No, don't tell me. Are you okay?

JUROR 6

No. Christ, no I'm not. Wait, we have to go through here.

MURDOCH

No, we have to go.

Too late – JUROR 6, braver now they're not alone, has gone to the side of the stage the FARMER vanished into, is peering cautiously beyond it.

JUROR 6

Nothing. There's nothing. But I saw it. I *heard* it.

MURDOCH

Don't say anything else, please.

They step off stage.

JUROR 6

(from offstage)

There's nothing. He's not here. But there was... Nothing.

*JUROR 6 comes back on stage. They look beaten,
bedraggled.*

*MURDOCH sees JUROR 6's pad on the floor, picks it
up and holds it out to them.*

MURDOCH

I don't know what you've seen or heard or experienced but
please, remember it. Just write it down. Now, let's go.

JUROR 6

Yes.

MURDOCH

Good. Come on, they're waiting for us.

*They leave the stage together, reappearing immediately
at the apron level where TIDYMAN, JUROR 4 and
JUROR 5 are waiting. As MURDOCH and JUROR
6 enter the cowshed to join them the noises of cows
fills the air – much louder and more insistent, with no
breaks. When characters speak, they struggle to hear each
other – except TIDYMAN.*

TIDYMAN

Is that the last of them?

MURDOCH

Yes.

JUROR 4

Then can we please go?

JUROR 5

Seconded.

JUROR 6

Now please. I want away from this place. Let's go somewhere light and built up and modern and full of electricity and concrete.

JUROR 4

You and us both, mate.

JUROR 5

Jesus, those cows are loud.

TIDYMAN

Pardon?

JUROR 5

The cows. Haven't they been fed, or milked, or whatever?

TIDYMAN

Cows?

MURDOCH

They don't bother you? He's right, they're getting loud. Maybe you've more of the country in you than you realise, Alice?

TIDYMAN

Bother me? Richard, there are no cows here. The farm closed after the incident and the livestock was sold. The place has been deserted ever since.

The sound of the cows rises to a crescendo as the lights drop, carrying on for a few seconds as the cast stands motionless. Cows suddenly snap off and the theatre is quiet. Cast exits.

Scene IX

Film projected on stage rear. Billowing mist, a young girl sitting, head down, in a plain room in front of floor length black curtains. Slowly, she stands up very slowly, raising her head and we see she has no eyes. Once upright, she stands motionless for perhaps twenty-five seconds and then very suddenly she screams.

EPILOGUE

All from stage.

MYERS is seated behind a desk. THE ACCUSED is standing on the side of the stage, TIDYMAN next to him. COLLINS is apart from them. All of COLLINS' next speech is from the front of the stage, making the audience the jury.

COLLINS

With the best will in the world, it's a nonsense. It's all a nonsense. With the greatest respect to Mrs Tidyman and Mr Murdoch, nothing that either has said or tried to show during this trial has changed the fundamental facts: that the accused broke in to the farm and killed the occupant, first by beating them and then by ending their life with a single blast from a shotgun. That the farmer was holding the shotgun should not be a surprise, given that the accused has already admitted to beating the victim. An attempt at self defence leading to a murder that, no matter how you approach it, cannot be called anything else but what it so clearly is: murder. And, again with the greatest respect to his academic credentials, nothing Mr Murdoch has told us here changes that. Ghosts. Really? The accused saw ghosts and was so frightened he mistook the victim as a ghost? No. This was a young man already stressed, breaking into a building where his own imagination and fears led to this tragic outcome. That none of the jurors saw the same things as each other in the farmhouse rooms is significant, and even if several of the stories appear to have similarities to the defendant's alleged visions we should read nothing into this. *You* should read nothing into this. There is one verdict to be reached, and one only. I ask you to do you duty and reach it.

COLLINS steps back. TIDYMAN steps forwards, also addressing the audience as the jury.

TIDYMAN

There's little more to say to round up this defence. My client admits everything he did but remains absolute in his statement that the environment he experienced at the farm was a major contributing factor to his actions. We've heard Mr Murdoch's arguments about the quiet places, that hauntings happen in the quietest places, and you've heard some of the statements he's gathered. You've heard the analysis of your own experiences in the crime scene and two other farms. It's clear that, whilst we are not claiming here to have proved the existence of ghosts or the afterlife, we have shown that *something* is clearly at work here. There's an atmosphere, an impact, of certain places on certain people that can influence behaviour and outcomes. I repeat: my client is not trying to avoid responsibility for his actions, only arguing that the accusation of murder is wrong. This was manslaughter, nothing more; a tragic, terrible outcome to a series of events that most of us cannot even begin to understand, but understand we must if we are to judge fairly. If there is even the hint of a doubt in your mind about the murder verdict, your duty is clear. You don't have to believe in ghosts to have those doubts, you just have to accept that there are quiet places in this world, quiet places that whisper and press and pry. Ladies and gentlemen of the jury, in your forthcoming discussions let your consciences be your guide.

Stage lights down. MURDOCH and TIDYMAN are illuminated by a single spotlight, alone together.

MURDOCH

Do you think—

TIDYMAN

I don't think. It is what it is. Either we've unseated their beliefs enough or we've not. Either he gets a lesser conviction or he doesn't. We did our best. You did your best, I did mine.

MURDOCH

But you? Do you believe?

TIDYMAN

What I believe doesn't matter. There's just the law, and justice, and decisions.

MURDOCH

I suppose.

TIDYMAN

I'll say again, Richard; you did your best. No one can ask for more.

MURDOCH

I just wonder if it's good enough.

TIDYMAN

It's all we have. Sometimes, it's all there is. For the record, I don't believe in ghosts, but I believe that there's something.

Spotlight off. Lights up. MYERS is still at the desk, the ACCUSED and TIDYMAN are together, COLLINS is apart. All are paying attention. MURDOCH is not there.

MYERS

Has the jury reached a verdict?

FOREMAN stands, centre of front row – they have been there throughout the entirety of the play.

FOREMAN

We have, your honour.

MYERS

And is the verdict unanimous?

FOREMAN

It is, your honour.

MYERS

So in the case of the crown versus the defendant, what is your verdict?

FOREMAN

We the jury find the defendant…

FOREMAN suddenly cut off by all lights suddenly snapping off. The FARMER'S final shriek plays again, cut off by a shotgun blast and a flash echoes around the theatre.

As the audience leaves, the girl with no eyes is somewhere in the foyer, lit blue from above. She may let out the occasional scream.

END

Afterword
On writing and performing a play

A disclaimer: the play you have just read is not the play that ended up being performed. I'll explain momentarily.

You could say this started with a bout of ill-advised day-drinking, or maybe it was with one of two bouts of stress-related burnout where I had to radically reconsider my life, or maybe it was the setting up of a side-hussle writing and leading historical ghost walks around the town where I live. We could go further than that and say it began at a story reading I was doing in Liverpool where I met Rosie, who later became my wife, or even further to two short story collections and three specific stories I wrote in 2010 and 2011. God knows where it began, but I know where it ended: May 11th 2024.

Ultimately, I blame the wine. Rosie and I were in a pub one afternoon celebrating a first successful ghost walk and drinking and talking about the next play she wanted to direct (coming off the back of having directed a successful version of Caryl Churchill's *Vinegar Tom* late last year) and couldn't decide what to tackle and I said, "Hell, I'll write you a ghost story!" And she said "Okay," so then I was committed… How hard could it be, I wondered? Ha. Let me tell you that writing for the stage, I very soon discovered, is very different from writing narrative fiction. You've only really got dialogue to move things along, and whilst I ended writing a lot of stage directions, they were being performed on the stage in my head and I had no idea what they'd look or sound like in a physical space. I was,

I realised, going to be at the mercy of the cast to sell this to the audience which, for a writer normally used to being the sole creator of the work, was a slightly odd and deeply unsettling experience.

In the end, I used three stories from my first two collections and the structure of my second, *Quiet Houses*, to create a portmanteau of ghost stories culminating in a (hopefully terrifying) climax set in a cowshed, wrote it to what I thought was the right length, and handed it over, assuming that my work was then done. At that point I had no plans to attend rehearsals, thinking that the director and cast could work out all the details themselves and not wanting to be in the position of hating any changes they might make especially as I sleep each night next to the director, but the universe (in the guise of Rosie) had other plans. She asked that I go to the first readthrough to read in the stage directions and answer any questions the prospective cast may have, which I did, and realised something straight away: what I thought were long, engaging chunks of dialogue were ... well ... a bit dull, and the whole thing (which I was convinced would be too short and would need an extra story adding) was way, *way* too long.

Editing stories and novels is easy, really – you listen to feedback, decide if you like it and change what needs changing. Editing the play proved far harder because suddenly I had to think about the cast, about who could say what, their strengths and the things they might not be comfortable with. And you're dealing with another person's interpretation of your characters which can change the tone and voice, sometimes in ways you'd never expect. One of the characters became a scouser on the stage without any input from me before the director thankfully intervened, one became a different gender and far younger than I intended, and one has entirely changed nationality.

Sexual tension between two of the characters was discussed because of the casting before being abandoned – probably a good thing but still fascinating from my perspective, as the original characters were never intended to look each other like *that*. All of these are good things, incidentally, because they forced me to look at the script in a way I'd not done before, not as its author but as an audience member responded to situations and characters and light and noises being played out before them. My job was then to shake it about and pull it and twist it and make it even better.

And then I got cast in it even though I initially didn't want to be. Four roles, only small and only two with lines, but it means I'm there at rehearsals and again, I was still editing as we went, seeing where things that worked well on the page were stuffy and slow on the stage, seeing where the terrifying "sticklike figure stalks across the stage" type of directions where practically impossible to pull off in real life so changing them, bringing them back within boundaries of what we could realistically achieve in a small theatre with a minimal budget, became a constant battle. The thing is, by this point the work was no longer mine: I was contributing not controlling, just like the rest of cast and, especially, the director and did they make decisions I didn't like? Yes. There are things I thought would work well, and still do, but a decision was made to do them differently and I had to accept that. On one level it was no different from editing text, a give and take between the professional editor and professional writer, only in this case the editor had, hydra-like, many heads and many voices. But for every edit that was made that I wish hadn't been there are two or three or four that I saw improving the work I first wrote. Keeping the ghost on stage instead of her leaving after that scene? Works better than my idea. Change the sound of wood tearing and wind roaring to a much subtler whirl of whispers? Oh, that's going to be so much more creepy. It's not easy, letting your words get changed by someone else, it never is, but when you can see the improvements those changes make it salves the burn a little and through it all I was immensely proud of my wife. Watching her get the best out of not just the cast but of the play itself was nothing short of awesome because she saw things and heard things I had never seen or heard and then knew how to change them up, to keep improving things. As a group, under her charge, we created something we could be entirely proud of and if it didn't look exactly like my initial idea well, thems the breaks.

So there it is. There's a play, and there's the performed piece, and they're different but their core elements are the same. If anyone else were to do this, I'm entirely sure that what they'd come up with would be different to what we managed to create, and still wouldn't exactly reflect the thing I wrote – and that's fine. Better than fine, it's great, because a play should always be a collaborative, evolving thing. Ignore the stage directions, change the dialogue, swap genders, add things. We did all that and more and you have my blessing to be as flexible as the original company were.

Some notes: in writing this, I wanted to make sure that no character was tied to any specific gender. I asked, for personal reasons, that Murdoch be cast male (Murdoch is called Nakata in the *Quiet Houses* story collection, and I've known him a very long time now and it felt important for him to still be a him) but every other character can be any gender they want and the casting director likes (although I always thought of the Accused as male, and always knew the ghost in the story was the protagonist's Mum and I'm not sure how well it'd work if, especially, the ghost became male). Additionally, the use of rear projections meant that we could get away with a minimal set – we ended using rear projections for every scene and dropping all the short movies except one, using images of empty attics and office bookshelves to create the impression of rooms. The aim was to keep everything as flexible as possible in the planning and early rehearsals so that we could end up at the best version of the play possible, and I think we achieved that. If you do ever perform this piece, the sound and visual effects can and should be changed to fit the cast and the physical environment its being performed in but the jump scares? Keep them, because some of them worked *really* well.

So now it's done, and all that's left are the memories and this script. Will I ever write another play? No, of course not, and I'm not going to be in one either, and I'm definitely not getting involved in trying to create visual or sound effects. Nope. Not me. Only, I've got this idea for a murder mystery and there's a special effect I know would be easy to do and that would work fantastically, and company really wants to tackle something I'm keen to adapt so maybe that 'no' isn't quite as resolute as it sounds.

Apparently, amongst other things, I'm a playwrite now. Let's see where it takes me…

Simon Kurt Unsworth
Kendal, May 2024

Quiet Hauntings was first performed at the Bryce Institute in Burneside on May 9th, 10th and 11th May 2024. The originating cast and crew were:

CAST

JUDGE MYERS	Samm Parker
THE ACCUSED	Ethan Brown
RICHARD MURDOCH	Chris Andrews
ALICE TIDYMAN	Rebecca de Villaneuve
JAMES COLLINS	Alex Knibbs
DANIELLE	Chloe Procter
ROB	Terry Cramphorn
THE HOTELIER	Dave Snow
A POLICEMAN	Simon Kurt Unsworth
THE WOMAN	Amelia Edwards
MEGAN	Sarah Edwards
ARNOST	Simon Kurt Unsworth
PEG	Chloe Procter
JUROR 1	Sarah Edwards
JUROR 2	Terry Cramphorn
JUROR 3	Samm Parker
JUROR 4	Ethan Brown
JUROR 5	Chloe Procter
JUROR 6	Dave Snow
FARMER	Simon Kurt Unsworth

CREW

Lighting	Ray Glenright
Sound	Nigel Cook
Sound Effects	Sebastian Raw
Visual Effects	Hartshead Productions Ltd.
Set Design	BATS Production Team
Costumes	Fran Milne
Props	The Eagle and Child, Stavely
Director	Rosie Seymour

This play is available to licence for performance. If you wish to discuss, this, please contact the publisher at contact@blackshuckbooks.co.uk in the first instance.

Milton Keynes UK
Ingram Content Group UK Ltd.
UKHW051912300624
444825UK00001B/10